This book belongs to

~~Alan~~ chris
Seller

Abraham Lincoln

By BELLA KORAL

Illustrated by JAY HYDE BARNUM
and JOHN ALAN MAXWELL

Prepared under the supervision of
JOSETTE FRANK
Reader's Adviser of the Child Study Association of America

RANDOM HOUSE · NEW YORK

Maxwell

IT was a cold wintry day. The wind howled down the chimney of the gray log cabin that stood in a small clearing in the Kentucky woods.

The wind blew hard and rattled the door on its leather hinge. But inside the cabin a great fire was blazing in the fireplace and all within were warm.

In the little log cabin lived Thomas Lincoln, his wife, Nancy, and their little daughter, Sally.

Now on this Sunday, the 12th of February, 1809, there was added to this family a new baby boy.

Little light came into the cabin through the oiled-paper window, but the happiness on the faces of the father and mother made the gloomy room seem bright.

Nancy Lincoln lay on her corn-husk mattress covered by a bearskin, with her new baby cuddled safely in her arm.

"We'll name him Abraham, after your father," she said to her husband. Thomas Lincoln was pleased. "Abe Lincoln," Nancy whispered to the baby.

Later that day, Dennis Hanks, Nancy's cousin, came in to visit the new baby. He had come running down the wilderness path from the cabin where he lived with his aunt and uncle.

Dennis tiptoed to the bed. "May I see him, Nancy?" he asked. Nancy smiled and turned back the cover. Dennis took a long look. "Why, he's red and wrinkly like dried cherry pulp," he said.

Next morning, when he and his Aunt Betsy came to help Nancy, Dennis wanted to hold little Abe.

"Be careful, Dennis," Nancy told him. "You're the first boy he's ever seen."

Dennis picked up the baby and rocked him in his arms. The baby screwed up its face, began to cry, and didn't stop.

Dennis gave him back quickly to his mother.

"Take him," he said in disgust. "He'll never 'mount to much."

Dennis could not have been more wrong—as he later found out —for that little baby, born in a log cabin, was to become one of the greatest men the world has ever seen.

As long as the earth lasts, his name and fame will not be forgotten!

In no time, Abe grew into a long-legged little fellow, with thick black hair and gray eyes. "He's as solemn as a papoose," said Dennis.

Abe, wearing the homespun petticoat that log cabin children wore, began following his father around as he worked in the corn field in front of the cabin. Soon he learned how to drop seeds into the furrows Thomas ploughed.

Abe's mother was quiet and gentle, and everyone who knew her loved her. Nancy was different from most women in the Kentucky settlements then, for she was able to read and write. She knew there was a great world outside where people lived and thought in ways different from those of folks around her. She dreamed that some day her children would see that world "out yonder."

Abe's father was an easy-going man, quiet and brave, too. He was a good carpenter, but loved his rifle better than his ax. Thomas

Maxwell

would rather track down a wild turkey for supper than build a cabin.
He liked to sit around and tell yarns and crack jokes.

He wasn't too fond of farming, either. So when he found his
corn and vegetables were not doing very well, he decided the ground
was too full of stumps and rocks, and looked for a new place to live.

When Abe was three the Lincoln family moved to Knob Creek farm.

The new cabin was just like the old one—built of rough logs cut from the forest near by. It was a one-room cabin with one door and one window, and a floor of packed-down earth.

There was a huge fireplace of stone and clay. It was so large that logs the size of a man could be rolled into it for a winter fire. Nancy Lincoln did all her cooking here. She stewed meat in a pot that hung from a swinging crane, and baked corn pones on a smooth plank on the hearth.

Nancy's spinning wheel and loom stood near the fireplace. Strings of dried apple, dried pumpkins and ears of corn hung from

the smoky boards of the roof.

The children slept on corn-husk mattresses on the floor. These were pushed under their parents' bed during the daytime.

When it was cold, Nancy Lincoln spread a bearskin rug before the fire for the children to sit on.

On clear nights Abe and Sally could look up from their corn-husk beds and see the stars twinkling down on them through the chinks in the roof.

Abe and Sally loved their home. It was the kind most of their neighbors lived in, too. Here the children played, and were happy.

Here, warmed by the love and courage of his parents, Abe grew and learned.

The farm at Knob Creek was the first home that Abe remembered. The Lincolns lived there till Abe was seven.

Knob Creek was still in the wilderness but it was on a big highway called the Louisville Pike. Many travelers passed there and covered wagons rumbled along by day and night, carrying people westward.

Traveling preachers and lawyers sometimes stopped at the Lincoln cabin for a meal or a night's rest.

Abe always listened as they talked of the world beyond the hills. He would ask questions and remember everything he heard.

The jingling bells of the peddler's cart driving along the highway every few months was music in Abe's ears. For the peddler would stop to chat and tell the news as he sold his pins and needles, and pots and pans.

Maxwell

Abe also used to look forward to the visits of Dr. Christopher Columbus Graham, a friend of the family. He was a scholar who studied the rocks, plants and animals of Kentucky.

After supper, Dr. Graham would open his bag to show the Lincolns the collection of dried flowers, snake skins, bright rocks and animal bones he was taking with him to Louisville to study and write about.

Hunters sometimes stopped at the cabin, too. Abe listened wide-eyed when one of them spoke of a big town named Washington, where the President of the United States lived. His eyes opened wider when the hunter told how the president and townspeople in Washington rode in coaches and ate off china plates.

And when Abe heard words like "freedom" and "slavery" he tried to figure out what they meant.

Once as Abe was trotting home with a little fish he had caught in the creek, he met a man on the Louisville Pike. The man wore a faded blue coat with brass buttons.

Abe's cap came off quickly. "Are you a soldier?" he asked.

"Yes," replied the man. "I've been with General Jackson and I fought through the war."

Abe's mother had taught him that he should always be kind to soldiers. His grandpa, Abraham Lincoln, for whom he was named, had been a soldier.

"Please take my fish," said Abe, putting it into the soldier's hand. "It'll make you a good supper." And off he ran.

There was plenty of work to do on Knob Creek farm. Mr. Lincoln had some horses, a cow, pigs and sheep. A boy could help a lot taking care of the animals, and Abe was a great help to his father.

Wearing his linsey-woolsey shirt, Abe rode a horse hitched to a "bull-tongue" plow. He helped his father plant corn, beans and potatoes and weeded the corn-patch till his hands were blistered.

Abe ran errands, carried pails full of water from the spring down the hill, and kept the wood-box filled with firewood.

He and his sister Sally picked currants and blueberries in the woods. Their mother spread them in the sun to dry and then put them away for winter. The children gathered walnuts and hickory nuts, and sometimes they found wild honey in "bee trees" before the bears got it.

Abe loved to go to Hodgen's Mill, eight miles away, to take a sackful of corn to be ground. He was strong and very tall for his age, so that he easily swung the corn sack onto his shoulders. At the mill he would meet and talk with other people from near-by settlements. There he could ask questions about the things that puzzled him.

To Abe Lincoln, the backwoods were a part of his home. He loved the forest and its creatures. Squirrels, birds and all the timid creatures that lived in the woods were his friends.

Abe's father taught him to pick up the sounds and warnings of the forest. He taught him to walk like an Indian, without making a sound. Sometimes Abe followed deer tracks to a forest pool. There, if he hardly breathed, he could watch a doe and her fawn with its turned-up perky white tail.

One day in March, when Abe was seven, Thomas Lincoln brought home exciting news. "Zachariah Riney is opening a school four miles up the pike!" he declared.

"The children will go, Thomas, won't they?" Nancy exclaimed, her eyes sparkling.

"Well, I don't know," Tom said. "I can't read nor write more than my name, still I get along. If Abe knows how to chop down trees and raise corn, that's enough," Tom went on.

"That's not enough for Abe, Thomas. He isn't like other boys. He asks so many questions about things," his wife answered.

"Abe asks too many questions. He ought to do more work," Mr. Lincoln replied.

"But Thomas, I've always wanted Abe and Sally to learn reading. Reading is *good!*" Nancy went on anxiously.

"Well, all right then, Nancy," Tom agreed. "I'll see Zachariah."

A few days later Abe and Sally were on their way to Master Riney's. Abe wore his homespun jacket and coonskin cap with the ringed tail flying out in a tassel. On his feet he wore clumsy bearskin moccasins his mother had made him, and he was very proud of his new deerskin breeches.

In those days there were no public schools or school houses in Kentucky, but parents would offer a schoolmaster the use of a deserted log cabin if he would open a school in it.

The settlers had little money, for they were poor. So they paid the schoolmaster by giving him meals or lodging or by washing his clothes.

Sally and Abe walked the wilderness path to the one-room cabin with the dirt floor where Master Riney kept his "blab" school. The only light came in through a space where one log had been left out of the wall.

The "blab" school was called that because all the pupils shouted their lessons out loud until it was time to recite.

The louder they shouted, the more sure the schoolmaster was that the children were working hard. A B C's and arithmetic tables and spelling words were all in the air at one time.

Mr. Riney stood, switch in hand, to see that no one was idle. He knew in a moment if a pupil stopped "blabbing" and went after that unlucky one with his switch.

Abe was the youngest pupil in the school. Most of the others were big boys and girls who had grown up without ever having seen books. Only a few could read.

One autumn evening when the family was at supper, Abe's father announced, "Kentucky is no place for us any more. Too many folks who own slaves are moving in."

Thomas and Nancy hated slavery. They would never live on other people's work. Nancy, besides, could not bear to hear of Negro mothers sold as slaves and sent so far away that they never saw their babies again.

"My brother Joe's moved to Indiana. It'll be a free state with no slavery allowed. And folks say there's rich corn land there, to be bought cheap," Tom went on. "So I reckon we'll move on to Indiana. What do you say, Nancy?"

Nancy answered quietly, "We'll do what you think is right, Thomas."

"When are we starting?" asked Abe excitedly.

"As soon as we can," replied Tom. "We must build us a shelter before the snow sets in."

Soon Abe's father set out alone to find their new home. He came back in a few weeks and the whole family packed and made ready for the long trip.

Early one December morning they piled their belongings on two horses. Sally and Nancy rode on one, and Abe and his father walked, leading the other horse over the rough roads.

After about a week they came to the wide Ohio River and crossed it by ferryboat. Then they were in Indiana. They had traveled almost a hundred miles.

"Just sixteen miles more before we reach that claim I set up," exclaimed Tom one day. But now they were in the deep forest. They had to hack a trail through dense woods so they could go on.

Abe worked with his father cutting down trees and brush to clear the way. And from now on—though he was only seven—the ax was scarcely ever out of his hands.

At last they reached the little clearing near Pigeon Creek where Tom planned to build his cabin.

"You have found a beautiful place, Thomas," said Nancy.

By now, winter was upon them, and they quickly set about building a shelter. It was a three-sided camp made of poles covered with leaves and brush.

The fourth side was a great open fireplace where a fire always burned.

The fire gave them warmth and kept away the howling wolves and other wild beasts of the forests. Over the fire Nancy cooked food for her family.

Sally and Nancy spread branches over the earthen floor and covered them with bearskins. Here the family slept during the long, cold winter.

Tom and Abe spent the days cutting down trees, hewing logs for the new cabin and clearing the land for a cornfield.

In the evenings, by the fire, Nancy sang or read from her Bible and Tom told stories. In the distance, they heard the howling wolves.

The new cabin was to be bigger and finer than their old one. "It'll have a loft for Abe to sleep in," Nancy said, "with pegs in the wall to climb up to it."

Spring came, then summer. The sound of axes rang through the woods as Abe and Tom worked away. Down came the great trees—to become logs for their new home.

One day Abe heard his father call, "Get up, Abe, the neighbors are coming for a house-raising. We'll sleep in our new cabin tonight."

All the neighbors for miles around were invited. Nancy and Sally cooked a dinner of wild turkey and green corn with stewed pumpkins and plum relish for the visitors and helpers.

That night, after the walls had been raised, and the roof put on with the help of many willing hands, the Lincolns decided to move right in. Even though the cabin was not finished, it seemed very fine after the pole-shed in which they had spent so many months.

Tom never did get around to laying the floor or putting in the window or door. There was too much good hunting—other things could wait.

More pioneers came to settle at Pigeon Creek, and Dennis Hanks was living with them now. Abe and Sally found it fun to have neighbors near by again. Abe was glad to hear there might soon be a school.

By the time Abe was going on nine, he was so tall he kept growing out of his breeches. He helped his father clear more land, chopping down trees, and burning logs. He could do almost a man's work with an ax.

Then came a terrible time. A strange illness broke out in the Pigeon Creek neighborhood. It struck at cattle and people, too.

Abe's mother nursed some of the sick neighbors and a few days later she became very ill. There was no doctor for many miles around. Her husband and the children did all they could to help, but Nancy grew worse each day.

When his mother died, Abe felt as if his whole world had ended. He would wander into the woods and think about the things she had told him. He missed the bright world she had opened up to him with her stories.

His father, too, was lonely and sad.

A year went by. The cabin became untidy, the children grew thinner and shabbier every day. Thomas Lincoln finally decided something must be done. He left for Kentucky. One day the children heard wagon wheels coming near. They ran out and saw a wagon piled high with furniture. Several children were in the wagon, too, and a woman was sitting on the seat beside their father.

Thomas had married a widow, Sarah Johnson, whom he had known as a young girl. Now she was here and had brought her own three children.

"Here's your new mammy," Thomas told Abe and Sally. They looked up at a tall, kind-faced woman who spoke to them in a warm and friendly voice.

The new Mrs. Lincoln's heart went out to these children in their dirty, ragged clothes. She saw in Abe's gray eyes his need for a mother's love. She held out her arms to him, and the boy went to her.

From then on his stepmother was, as Abe later said, "the best friend he had."

Soon the big wagon was unloaded. There were real chairs with backs, there were featherbeds, pillows, quilts and a shining bureau of dark smooth wood.

How the new stepmother worked to make everything tidy! Everything was scrubbed and cleaned—the children, too, until they couldn't be cleaner.

It was good to sit down to a warm supper with eight around the table!

That night Dennis and Abe slept on featherbeds in their loft, with soft, fluffy pillows under their heads.

After a while the cheerless cabin became homelike with a wooden floor, windows and a door. Mrs. Lincoln also had her husband whitewash the walls and ceiling. The new mother brought sunshine where there had been sadness and loneliness.

Sarah Lincoln saw that Abe was not like other children. She came to understand his deep thirst for learning, and tried to help him all she could. Abe, in turn, loved her dearly.

When there were enough settlers at Pigeon Creek, a school was started and Mrs. Lincoln saw that Abe went, even though Thomas kept saying it was a waste of time. The school, nine miles away, lasted only a few weeks, but Abe learned to write. He had no pencil, so he used charcoal. He had no paper or slate, so he wrote on a wooden shovel. When he had covered it with writing, he would shave it off, to have a smooth clean place to write again. The Lincolns had no candles, so Abe would lie in front of the fire and study by its light.

When Abe was able to get some paper, later on, he made himself a pen out of a turkey quill. For ink he used the juice of wild berries. With his homemade pen and ink he wrote his first composition—an essay against cruelty to animals.

Abe went to school twice more at Pigeon Creek, each time for only a few weeks. When he was a grown man, he said, "I went to school by littles, and all my school life didn't amount to more than a year."

Sarah was proud of Abe and told the neighbors how hard he studied. Soon, if anyone in the settlement had a book, Abe was welcome to borrow it. He would walk miles to get it and would read it far into the night till he knew it by heart.

He would take a book with him when he went ploughing and read while he rested his horse at the end of each furrow.

Once Abe walked a long distance to borrow a book called *The Life of George Washington* from a farmer named Crawford. He read while he was walking home and took the book up with him to the loft where he slept. He tucked it between two logs in the wall, for he was going to read again when dawn came.

During the night a storm came up and the rain drove in between the logs. The book was wet through and the covers spoiled. Abe dried the pages as well as he could, and finished reading the book.

Then, with a heavy heart, he returned the book to Mr. Crawford. He explained how the accident had happened, and how sorry he was.

"Well, Abe," said the farmer, "this book meant a lot to me, but I suppose it was an accident. If you want to make up for it, come and work three days in my cornfield."

So for three days, from sunrise to sunset, Abe gathered fodder in Mr. Crawford's cornfields to pay for the damage to the book.

Then Abe had a wonderful surprise. Mr. Crawford *gave* him the book! He walked home, the happiest of boys, for Washington was Abe's great hero. More and more he was going to try to be like Washington, the first President.

Abe was growing so fast that Mrs. Lincoln joked with him about keeping his head clean so he wouldn't dirty her whitewashed ceiling. "I can scrub the floor," she said laughingly, "so I don't mind your bringing dirt in on your *feet!*"

Abe loved a joke, and that afternoon, when his stepmother was away visiting a neighbor, Abe thought of one to play on her.

Calling to one of the barefooted boys playing in a puddle in the road, he said, "Danny, how'd you like a walk on the ceiling?"

Danny saw there was fun a-brewing. In a moment Abe had carried the little fellow into the house upside down and had him

make muddy tracks across the ceiling.

When Mrs. Lincoln came home, Danny was hiding, and Abe was reading. Mrs. Lincoln looked at him proudly. He would amount to something some day.

Then she happened to glance up at the ceiling. "Abe!" she gasped. But when she saw the mischief in his face she burst out laughing. Danny came out, and they all laughed till they had tears in their eyes. Then Abe whitewashed the ceiling again till it looked like new.

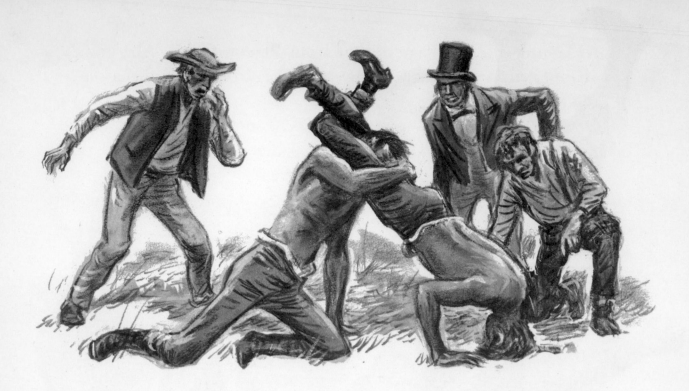

Besides helping his father on the farm, Abe earned extra money by working as farm hand for the neighbors, and splitting rails for their fences. By the time he was seventeen, he was six feet four inches tall. "Why, that lanky Abe is as strong as three men," said a farmer.

One day four men were trying to move a chicken coop weighing six hundred pounds. Young Abe came along and said, "Where do you want that?" The men pointed. While they stood open-mouthed, he got under the coop and carried it to the new spot.

By that time Abe was the best wrestler in several counties. And he was the best runner and jumper too. Still, day and night, whenever he could, Abe kept on studying and reading.

Sometimes, out in the fields, he would recite from memory speeches he had learned from his books. Farm boys from near-by fields would come running to hear them and to hear Abe tell funny stories.

Once, when this happened while Abe was working at the Crawfords' during harvest time, Mrs. Crawford asked him, "What's going to become of you, Abe?"

"Why, ma'am," he answered, half joking, but half in earnest, "I'm going to be President—leastways I'll study and get ready."

At Gentryville, a village not far from Pigeon Creek, Abe got a job at Jones' store. He also ran the ferryboat from the Indiana side of the Ohio River.

One day, two men who ran the ferry from the Kentucky side, brought Abe to court before a Kentucky judge.

"He's from Indiana," they complained, "and has no right ferrying people across the river to Kentucky. It's against the law!"

The judge asked Abe if he had taken passengers out beyond the middle of the river. Abe answered, "No, sir, I only ferry them as far as the steamboats in the middle of the river."

"Then," said the judge to the men, "he's not breaking the law."

The judge's words gave Abe a new idea—a new direction in life. Here was something he was going to learn about!

As often as he could, he went to the courtroom to listen to the Kentucky judge. From another judge Abe borrowed a book about Indiana laws. In this book he found the Constitution of the United States and The Declaration of Independence in which it was stated that "All men are created equal."

Abe thought about what he learned in the law books and talked about these things with people who came into the store. They loved to listen to him, for with a funny story he helped to make the law simple and clear to himself and them.

When Andrew Jackson became President, there was great excitement among the folks in Gentryville. A man who had been a farm boy, like many of them, had reached the highest place in the land.

The country was growing fast with settlers spreading out 'way beyond the Mississippi. As a river boatman, Abe met all kinds of travelers who opened his mind to new ideas.

Now came a chance for Abe to see something of the world. He was hired by Mr. Gentry to go with his son Allen down the Mississippi River by flatboat (a kind of raft) to New Orleans. There they were to sell a load of farm products.

(When Lincoln was young, there were no railroads and goods had to be carried either by wagon or by boat.)

The trip was a thousand miles down waters where Abe, who steered the flatboat, had to watch out for rocks, uprooted trees and changing currents. He had to keep out of the paths of the huge paddle-wheel steamers so as not to be sucked into the waters.

At night they tied up near the shore. Abe and Allen took turns standing on watch to see that their cargo was not stolen by river pirates.

One night, near the end of the trip, seven river pirates boarded the boat. Allen's shouts awakened Abe. Swinging his crab-tree club, that young giant lashed out at the thieves, landing mighty blows.

The pirates were only too glad to escape into the woods, but Abe carried a scar over his eye for the rest of his life as a reminder of the fight.

New Orleans was the first large city Abe had ever seen. He and Allen wandered through its narrow streets, staring at the pretty houses with their lacy iron balconies. They saw richly dressed people riding in carriages, and sailors from many lands.

One thing that Abe saw he never forgot. Like the scar he had gotten in the fight with the pirates, it stayed with him always.

In a big market place white men were selling Negro men, women, and children. Slave buyers from southern plantations were looking over these Negroes, feeling their muscles and counting their teeth to see if they were strong and healthy.

Wives were torn from husbands, and children from mothers, never to see each other again.

Abe's lips trembled and tears came into his eyes. He knew that slavery was not against the law. And later, he said, "If ever I get a chance to hit that, I'll hit it hard."

The law said slavery *was* allowed in states below the Ohio River. It was not allowed in the Northern states.

In the South, where slave-owning was allowed, plantation owners had bought thousands and thousands of Negroes. Some worked as servants, but most of them were used as field hands on their masters' great cotton and sugar plantations.

Many slave owners treated their slaves cruelly, though some slaves were given good care by their masters. But no slave knew when he might be sold to a master far away, and be separated from his family forever.

Back in Indiana, Abe found his father ready to move again. Thomas had heard of great prairies along the Sangamon River in Illinois where farming was scarcely any work at all. Sangamon was an Indian word meaning "land of plenty to eat" and Thomas hoped that was what it would prove to be.

In early spring the Lincolns with all their children (all were married now but Abe) started out in a great caravan. A covered wagon, drawn by four yoke of oxen led by Abe, carried their belongings. The men walked, while the women rode. Sometimes the wagon sank deep in the mud. Then all hands had to help lift it out.

One day they crossed a small river full of floating ice. When they were over, they heard a dog barking on the shore they had just left. It was their own dog, afraid to swim through the ice. Back and forth he ran, whining pitifully.

Abe couldn't bear to leave him behind. Plunging into the water, he waded across and picked up the shivering animal. "That's all right, boy," said Abe as the dog, yelping for joy, licked his face.

Abe helped his father build another cabin in the new country.

Now he was twenty-one, and Abe felt it was time to strike out for himself. Saying goodby to his parents, he put his arms about his stepmother and held her close. "I'll never forget you, Mother, and all you've done for me," he said.

Abe found plenty of work with neighbors. He made a bargain with one of them, a Mrs. Miller, who wove more jeans cloth for trousers than her menfolk could use. "I'll split four hundred fence rails for you, for every yard of your jeans cloth," Abe offered.

"That's a bargain," agreed Mrs. Miller. "I'll make you the jeans." Since Abe's long legs took lots of cloth to cover them, Abe split fourteen hundred rails to pay for his trousers.

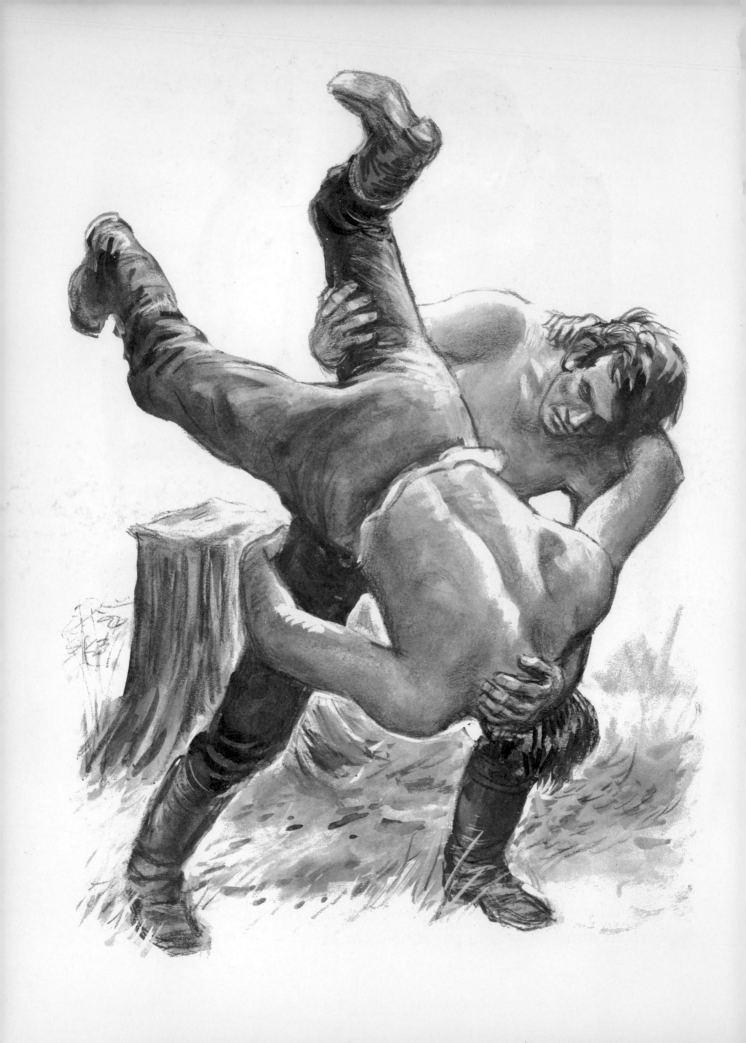

At about this time Abe met a man named Offut who asked him to be the clerk in his store in New Salem, a village on the Sangamon.

It wasn't long before Offut was boasting all over the place about his young clerk. "That Abe knows more than any other man in this country! He's going to be President, I'll bet, and what's more, he can outwrestle anybody in the country!"

A group of rough young men called the Clary Grove Boys took up Offut's dare. A wrestling match was arranged between Abe and their strongest man, Jack Armstrong.

Armstrong was built like a bull, but Abe's arms were strong as iron. Before a crowd that gathered from miles around, Abe easily held Jack off. Then Jack lost his temper and wrestled unfairly. Lincoln picked him up, shook him, and then pinned him to the ground.

Armstrong's friends were all ready to attack Abe when they were called off by their leader. "Abe's all right, boys," Jack said. "He fought fair. Let's shake hands."

From then on Abe was their friend. They respected and liked him, not only because he was strong, but because they found he was always on the side of right and justice.

At Offut's store Abe made many more friends who enjoyed his funny stories and liked him for his good nature. But it was his honesty that they talked about most.

One day by mistake Abe gave a woman less tea than she had paid for. When he discovered this, he walked four miles to give her the tea he owed her. Such deeds earned him the nickname of "Honest Abe," and by that name he was known as long as he lived.

Abe kept on studying while he worked for Offut. The village schoolmaster told Abe that a grammar would help him learn to speak and write good English. That very night Abe walked twelve miles to borrow one and was not satisfied till he had learned everything in it.

After a while Offut had to close his shop, for he was not a good business man. Now Abe was without a job.

Just then news came that Black Hawk, an Indian chief, was leading his braves on the warpath back into their old hunting grounds in Illinois. The Indians wanted back the lands they had sold to white settlers. They were attacking some settlements.

The men of New Salem, among them the Clary Grove Boys, formed a company to drive the Indians back. Abe was very proud when they picked him to be their captain!

Captain Abe led his men to war, but the war was over before they had a chance to fight, for Black Hawk was soon taken prisoner.

One day a half-starved old Indian came to the camp with a message saying he was a friend. Abe's men would not believe this and said he was a spy. They were ready to shoot him, but Abe said, "Anyone who dares harm him must answer to me!"

The men released the Indian. They knew how strong Abe was! And then they found that the Indian had told the truth.

Soon after Abe's return from the war, he opened a store with a man named Berry. Friends who trusted "Honest Abe" lent him money.

Berry was a lazy, wasteful man—and Abe loved books and people too much to be a real business man.

Once a family going west in a covered wagon stopped at his store. They asked Abe to buy a barrel of old things they couldn't use. Abe couldn't use the things either, but the people looked hungry, so he gave them fifty cents for the lot.

Later, to his delight, he found in the barrel an important law book he had long wanted. Now he would stretch out on the store counter and read, or lie under a tree outside, studying and thinking.

It was not long before the store failed. Berry died and Abe was left to pay the debt they both owed. Abe felt Berry's debt was his, too. It took him years, but in the end "Honest Abe" paid back every penny.

Abe took many jobs around the settlement. Again the woods rang to the sound of his ax splitting rails for farmers. Then he became postmaster, and could read the newspapers coming in by mail. Later he became a surveyor.

Lincoln made friends wherever he went. People enjoyed listening to him. "If you want to know anything about politics," they would say, "go and ask Abe."

That fall they elected Abe to be their representative in the legislature at Springfield, the state capital of Illinois.

Lincoln arrived in Springfield with only the few things he owned in a pair of saddlebags on a borrowed horse. Springfield would be his home for many years.

An old friend, Josh Speed, invited Abe to use a little room above his store, for Abe was penniless. Another friend advised him about his law studies so that Lincoln was soon able to pass the test to become a lawyer. They set up a law office as partners, and Abe was elected three times to the legislature.

Lincoln was popular and was invited to many gatherings. At one of these he met a young lady, Mary Todd from Kentucky, who was visiting Springfield. She was pretty and smart, with a saucy way of talking.

Many young men admired her. Among them was the well-known lawyer, Stephen A. Douglas, who was plump and short and on his way to fame. Of them all, Mary chose lank and awkward Abe.

Mary had told her friends, "I've always told you, the man I marry will be President of the United States!" She had a feeling Abe would some day be famous, and she made up her mind to help him.

After they were married they lived in a small house that Mary furnished in style. Mary kept house and took care of the three little boys that were born to them in the next few years.

The boys were lively and noisy. They liked nothing better than to tumble and climb all over their father when he tried to read in his favorite position—lying stretched out on the parlor floor in his stocking feet.

Mrs. Lincoln wished Abe would behave like the important man he was, for she was proud of him. When he answered the doorbell in his shirt-sleeves, or forgot to button his vest, she would scold him.

Lincoln spent many months of the year as a traveling lawyer. "Riding the circuit," it was called. It meant that a group of judges and lawyers rode from town to town, trying cases in the courts.

Jogging over the countryside on "Old Buck," his horse, Lincoln became known and loved far and wide. Courts were crowded when he appeared.

Many people hired Lincoln as their lawyer when they were in trouble, for he would state their cases so wisely that he usually won.

One such case was that of Duff, son of his old friend, Jack Armstrong, whom Lincoln had beaten in that wrestling match years before.

Duff was accused of killing a man. The main witness against him swore he had seen Duff do it. Said the witness, "The moon was shining so bright, I could see as if it was daylight."

"Are you *sure* the moon was shining?" asked Lincoln. The man nodded boldy.

Lincoln whipped an almanac out of his pocket. Now an almanac tells the part of each month when the moon can be seen.

Lincoln showed the judge and jury that the moon could *not* have been shining that night, and so proved the witness was telling a lie. It turned out that *he*, and not Duff, was the killer.

Abe's heart reached out not only to people but even to the smallest creatures.

One day some lawyers were riding to court on horseback, two by two along a lane. Lincoln was in the rear. As they passed some crabapple trees, they heard a loud fluttering and chirping overhead. From down in the grass came feeble little "peeps."

"I suppose last night's storm blew a couple of robins out of their nest," said one of the lawyers. "They're too young to fly and the mother robin's making a great fuss."

The lawyers rode on, laughing and talking. That is, all but Lincoln. He got off his horse and picked up the tiny birds. They chirped softly. Their nest was high up in the tree, but Abe had climbed many a tree. Soon the little family were all happily together again in the nest.

Lincoln, his coat ripped, rejoined his friends. They teased him for worrying about the robins. But he replied, "I couldn't have slept tonight if I'd left those helpless little birds to die in the grass."

The years rolled along and great changes were taking place. Railroads were spreading over the land and great cities were growing up across the country. Yet slavery and the cruel slave trade were still going on.

And now a great argument was arising in the country as new states came into the growing Union.

The Northern States did *not* want the new states to be allowed to have slavery, while the Southern States *did* want them to be allowed to have slavery.

In the meantime Stephen A. Douglas, the man who had admired Mary Todd years before, had become famous throughout the country.

He was called "The Little Giant" and thought *he* had found the right answer. "Let the people of each state," he said, "decide for themselves whether their state shall have slavery or not." Douglas traveled through Illinois stating his plan.

Now, at last, Lincoln came forward. He knew the question could never be decided that way. "The Nation cannot go on forever *half* slave and *half* free," he declared. It would have to be all one or all the other.

Wherever Douglas spoke, Lincoln also spoke. These arguments on both sides of this great question were called "debates."

From the prairies and towns of Illinois great crowds came to hear these debates between "The Little Giant" and "Abe, the Giant Killer," as they called Lincoln. People came afoot, on horseback, in covered wagons, and by train.

They camped on fields and hillsides. The debates were like huge picnics with parades, brass bands, and floats. One float was a long wagon, drawn by sixteen yoke of oxen, with men on it splitting rails. Its banner read, "We're for Abe, the Railsplitter."

Lincoln appeared on the speakers' platform in his stove-pipe hat and baggy suit. How dapper the small Mr. Douglas looked in his ruffled shirt and neatly buttoned coat!

Douglas tried never to say anything that might offend people who believed Negro slavery should go right on. He wanted their votes.

But Lincoln spoke in clear, honest words that rang out over the land, for he believed Negroes had as much right to be free as other Americans.

The debates made Lincoln famous. People in the East were eager to hear this man who had been an Indiana backwoods boy.

In New York, where he spoke, his words sank deep into men's hearts. People sprang to their feet, cheering him wildly.

A new party, the Republican Party, was formed by men who thought slavery was wicked and should not be allowed to spread.

Before long important men of this party called on Lincoln to tell him he had been chosen to run for President. Douglas and two other men were chosen by other parties.

Torchlight parades were held in the cities, night after night. "We want 'Honest Abe' for President," roared crowds of Republicans. The marchers carried fence rails in honor of Lincoln, the railsplitter.

Hundreds of letters arrived for Lincoln—one from a little girl. "Please let your beard grow, Mr. Lincoln," she wrote. "It would make you so much handsomer." Lincoln enjoyed her letter, and busy as he was, wrote her a reply. And what's more, he *did* let his beard grow!

When the returns came in showing he had won, Lincoln rushed home through the cheering crowds. "Mary, we've been elected!" he shouted. Their dreams had come true. Mary's husband was to be President of the United States.

Before he left for Washington Lincoln visited his stepmother, who still lived in the cabin Abe had helped build so long ago. "I'm proud of you, Abe," she said, as he kissed her good-bye.

It was a dark and rainy morning when Abe left for Washington, but the station was filled with old friends and neighbors who came to say farewell. Lincoln, wearing his tall silk hat and a fringed shawl about his shoulders, shook hands with his well-wishers.

"Good-bye, God bless you, Abe," they called. The train pulled out, slowly gathering speed.

Abe was going to the great task before him. Years of suffering and sorrow for himself and the nation lay ahead. But Lincoln's mission could not, and would not, fail. His great heart and courage would endure.

He would keep the country united and preserve the Union. With a ringing Proclamation he would wipe out slavery, and prove to the whole world that "government of the people, by the people, and for the people" would not perish from the earth.

RANDOM HOUSE BOOKS FOR CHILDREN

Question and Answer Books

For ages 6-10:
Question and Answer Book of Nature
Question and Answer Book of Science
Question and Answer Book of Space
Question and Answer Book About the
    Human Body

Gateway Books

For ages 8 and up:
The Friendly Dolphins
The Horse that Swam Away
Champ: Gallant Collie
Mystery of the Musical Umbrella
and other titles

Step-Up Books

For ages 7-8:
Animals Do the Strangest Things
Birds Do the Strangest Things
Fish Do the Strangest Things
Meet Abraham Lincoln
Meet John F. Kennedy
and other titles

Babar Books

For ages 4 and up:
The Story of Babar
Babar the King
The Travels of Babar
Babar Comes to America
and other titles

Books by Dr. Seuss

For ages 5 and up:
Dr. Seuss's Sleep Book
Happy Birthday to You!
Horton Hatches the Egg
Horton Hears a Who
If I Ran the Zoo
I Had Trouble in Getting to Solla
    Sollew
McElligot's Pool
On Beyond Zebra
Scrambled Eggs Super!
The Sneetches
Thidwick: The Big-Hearted Moose
Yertle the Turtle
and other titles

Giant Picture Books

For ages 5 and up:
Abraham Lincoln
Big Black Horse
Big Book of Things to Do and
    Make
Big Book of Tricks and Magic
Blue Fairy Book
Daniel Boone
Famous Indian Tribes
George Washington
Hiawatha
King Arthur
Peter Pan
Robert E. Lee
Robin Hood
Robinson Crusoe
Three Little Horses
Three Little Horses at the King's
    Palace

Beginner Books

For ages 5-7:
The Cat in the Hat Beginner Book
    Dictionary
The Cat in the Hat
The Cat in the Hat Comes Back
Dr. Seuss's ABC Book
Green Eggs and Ham
Go, Dog, Go!
Bennett Cerf's Book of Riddles
The King, the Mice and the Cheese
and other titles

Picture Books

For ages 4 and up:
Poems to Read to the Very Young
Songs to Sing with the Very Young
Stories to Read to the Very Young
Alice in Wonderland
Anderson's Fairy Tales
Bambi's Children
Black Beauty
Favorite Tales for the Very Young
Grandmas and Grandpas
Grimm's Fairy Tales
Heidi
Little Lost Kitten
Mother Goose
Once-Upon-A-Time Storybook
Pinocchio
Puppy Dog Tales
Read-Aloud Nursery Tales
Sleeping Beauty
The Sleepytime Storybook
Stories that Never Grow Old
The Wild and Wooly Animal Book
The Wizard of Oz

RANDOM HOUSE, INC., 457 MADISON AVENUE, NEW YORK 22, N.Y.